Move Over!

By Janine Amos   Illustrated by Annabel Spenceley
Consultant Rachael Underwood

Gareth Stevens Publishing
A WORLD ALMANAC EDUCATION GROUP COMPANY

Please visit our web site at: www.garethstevens.com
For a free color catalog describing Gareth Stevens Publishing's
list of high-quality books and multimedia programs, call
1-800-542-2595 (USA) or 1-800-387-3178 (Canada).
Gareth Stevens Publishing's fax: (414) 332-3567.

Library of Congress Cataloging-in-Publication Data

Amos, Janine.
    Move over! / by Janine Amos; illustrated by Annabel Spenceley.
      p. cm. — (Courteous kids)
    Includes bibliographical references.
    Summary: Two brief stories demonstrate that people can feel cramped and angry
when they do not have enough space, and the importance of looking for more space
when it is needed.
    ISBN 0-8368-3610-3 (lib. bdg.)
    1. Social interaction in children—Juvenile literature. 2. Problem solving in children—
Juvenile literature. [1. Problem solving. 2. Behavior. 3. Etiquette. 4. Conduct of life.]
I. Spenceley, Annabel, ill. II. Title.
BF723.S62A474 2003
177'.1—dc21   2002036475

This edition first published in 2003 by
Gareth Stevens Publishing
A World Almanac Education Group Company
330 West Olive Street, Suite 100
Milwaukee, Wisconsin 53212 USA

Series editor: Dorothy L. Gibbs
Graphic designer: Katherine A. Goedheer
Cover design: Joel Bucaro

This edition © 2003 by Gareth Stevens, Inc. First published by Cherrytree Press,
a subsidiary of Evans Brothers Limited. © 1999 by Cherrytree (a member of the
Evans Group of Publishers), 2A Portman Mansions, Chiltern Street, London
W1U 6NR, United Kingdom. This U.S. edition published under license from
Evans Brothers Limited. Additional end matter © 2003 by Gareth Stevens, Inc.

Printed in the United States of America

1 2 3 4 5 6 7 8 9 07 06 05 04 03

Note to Parents and Teachers

The questions that appear in **boldface** type can be used to initiate
discussion with your children or class. Encourage them to think of
possible answers before continuing with the story.

The Tent

Farid is in the tent.

Here comes Lily.

Now Farid and Lily are both in the tent.

Here come Jack and Sarah.

Farid and Lily and Jack and Sarah
are all in the tent.

Here comes Sam.

Sam squeezes into the tent.
How do you think the others feel?

"Move over!" Jack grumbles.
"I'm squashed."

"I'm squashed, too," says Lily.
What do you think she could do?

Lily crawls out of the tent.

Then she gets two chairs.

"I need this rug," Lily says.
"Please, help me, Sam."

Lily and Sam make another tent.

With two tents, everyone has enough room.

Oh, dear! Here comes Peter!

The Rocket

Jamie is building a rocket.
The table is covered with boxes.

"Hey! Move over!" says Nathan.
"I need more space."

21

Jamie plays with his rocket.
"Zoom! Zoom!" he says.

"Move over!" Nathan shouts, and
he pushes Jamie's boxes onto the floor.

"What's going on?" asks Steve.
"You two look upset."

"Nathan pushed my boxes off the table," says Jamie.
How do you think Jamie feels?

"Jamie is taking up the whole table,"
says Nathan. "There's no room for me."
How do you think Nathan feels?

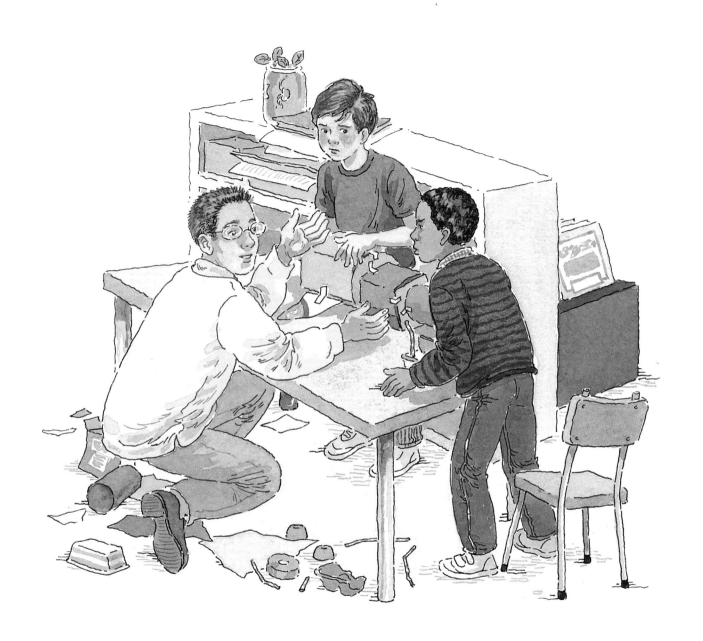

"So you both need more space," says Steve.
What do you think they could do?

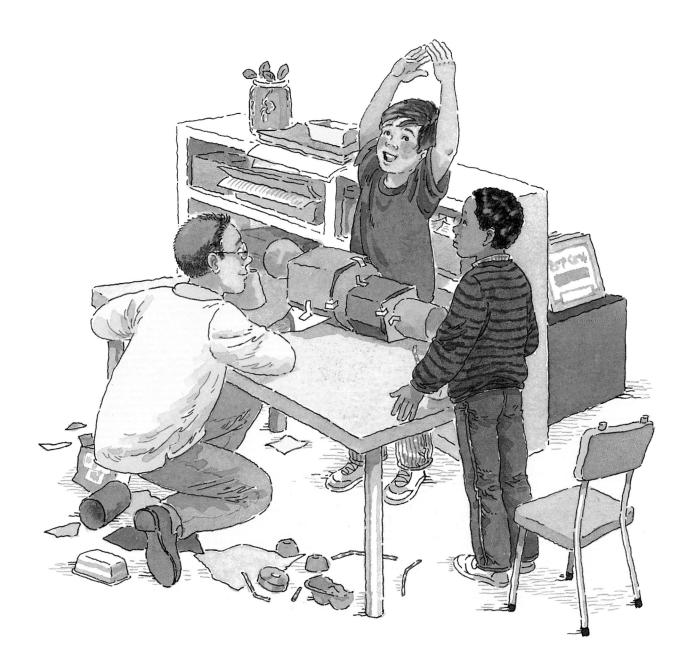

"I've got a good idea," says Jamie.
"I could build my rocket upward."

"Show me," says Steve.
Jamie stands his rocket up on one end.

Nathan smiles.
"Look! There's space for me now!" he says.

Jamie finishes his rocket.
Nathan makes his model.

31

When people don't have enough space to work or play, they feel crowded and, sometimes, they get angry. When you feel crowded and need more space, stop and look around. Try to find a way to make the space you need. You could even ask another person to help you.

More Books to Read

Dealing with Someone Who Is Selfish.
Don Middleton (PowerKids Press)

I Am Cooperative. Character Values (series).
Sarah L. Schuette (Pebble Books)

Room on the Broom. Julia Donaldson
(Dial Books for Young Readers)